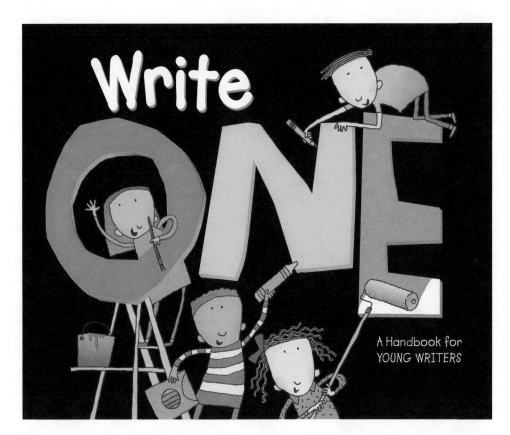

Write ONE

A Handbook for YOUNG WRITERS

Authors **Dave Kemper, Carol Elsholz, Patrick Sebranek**
Illustrator **Chris Krenzke**

WRITE SOURCE®

GREAT SOURCE EDUCATION GROUP
a Houghton Mifflin Company
Wilmington, Massachusetts

Acknowledgements

We're grateful to many people who helped bring *Write One* to life. First, we must thank all the students who contributed their writing models and ideas. Also, thanks to the writers, editors, and teachers who helped make this book a reality.

Betty Anderson   Nancy Koceja
Jane Barbian   Carol Luoma & team
Betsey Bystol   Dian Lynch
Dana Callen   Deb Pingle
Sharon Frost   Jacqueline Scholze

In addition, we want to thank our Write Source/Great Source team for all their help: Laura Bachman, Heather Bachman, Colleen Belmont, Liz DiBenedetto, Sandra Easton, Sherry Gordon, Bev Jessen, Lois Krenzke, Ellen Leitheusser, Shiere Melin, Tina Miller, Sue Paro, Allyson Shifley, Teresa Smet, Richard Spencer, and Sandy Wagner.

I(T)P® International Thomson Publishing
The ITP logo is a trademark under licence
www.thomson.com

Copyright © 1999 by Great Source Education Group, Inc., a Houghton Mifflin Company. All rights reserved. First published by Great Source Education Group, Inc., a Houghton Mifflin Company. All rights reserved.

Published in Canada in 1999 by

I(T)P® Nelson

A division of Thomson Canada Limited
1120 Birchmount Road
Scarborough, Ontario M1K 5G4
www.nelson.com

Canadian Cataloguing in Publication Data

Kemper, Dave
    Write one : a handbook for young writers

For use in grade 1.
Includes index.
ISBN 0-17-618660-3

1. English language — Composition and exercises — Juvenile literature.
I. Elsholz, Carol. II. Sebranek, Patrick. III. Title.

LB1576.K453 1999   808'.042   C98-932946-1

Printed and bound in Canada
1 2 3 4 5 6 7 8 9 0 /ML/ 7 6 5 4 3 2 1 0 9

Write One . . .
You'll Have Fun!

The *Write One* handbook has four parts:

The Process of Writing This part tells you all about being a writer.

The Forms of Writing In this part you'll learn about writing notes, stories, poems, and more.

Reading and Word Study Here you'll learn the letter sounds and how to read and write new words.

The Student Almanac This part has pictures, names of animals and places, maps, math charts, and lots more.

Table of Contents

The **Process** of Writing

All About Writing

Rules for Writing

4

The **Forms** of Writing

Personal Writing

Subject Writing

Research Writing

Story and Poetry Writing

Reading and Word Study

Reading Skills

Word-Study Skills

6

The Student **Almanac**

Helpful Words, Maps, and Lists

The **Process** of Writing

All About Writing

Jenny and her friends discover that being writers is exciting. You can learn more and more about the writing process every time you write.

Jenny Writes

It's writing time in Room 101. Luke is planning a story. Rosa is writing a poem. And Ben is writing something silly.

Jenny wonders, "What can I write?"

11

Jenny asks Luke what he's writing.
Luke tells her he's writing a dog story.
It's about his three big dogs. Luke
knows a lot about dogs.

Jenny wonders again, "What can I write?"

13

Jenny asks Rosa about her poem.
Rosa reads it to Jenny. It's about the
time she went fishing with her grandpa.
Rosa's poem rhymes.

Jenny still wonders, "What can I write?"

15

Then Ben pops up next to Jenny's desk.
Ben shows her the silly note he wrote. Jenny
and Ben laugh at the note.

Suddenly Jenny thinks, "This note gives me an idea."

Just like her friends, Jenny begins to write and draw.

Jenny writes a note to her mom and dad.

Hi Mom and Dad,
I like cats.
Luke has three
BIG DOGS!
I wish we had
one little cat.

Love,
Jenny

19

Being a Writer

Being a writer means you do special things.

GATHER your materials—paper, pencils, and art materials.

WRITE about things you know about.

LEARN to use the writing process.

FIND ways to spell words.

- Say the words slowly and listen for sounds in the beginning, middle, and end.

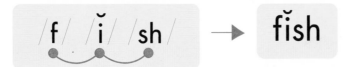 → fĭsh

- Look for words in your classroom.

word walls   word books   posters

- Ask others for help.

SHARE your writing with others.

Hi Mom and Dad,
I like cats.
Luke has three
BIG DOGS!
I wish we had
one little cat.

Love,
Jenny

21

Steps in the Writing Process

The **writing process** has five steps: planning, writing, revising, checking, and publishing.

I

PLAN

- Talk.
- Draw.
- Think.
- Write lists.

Things Pets Need

1. food
2. water
3. love
4. a plas to sleep
5. toys

22

2

WRITE

- Write sentences about the topic.
- Spell words the best you can.
- Use your plan as you write.

Things Pets Need

Pets need food and water. Pets like to be loved. they need a plas to sleep. Pets like to have toys.

23

3

REVISE

- Read it aloud.
- Does it sound right?
- Make changes.

4

CHECK

- Capitals
- Punctuation
- Spelling

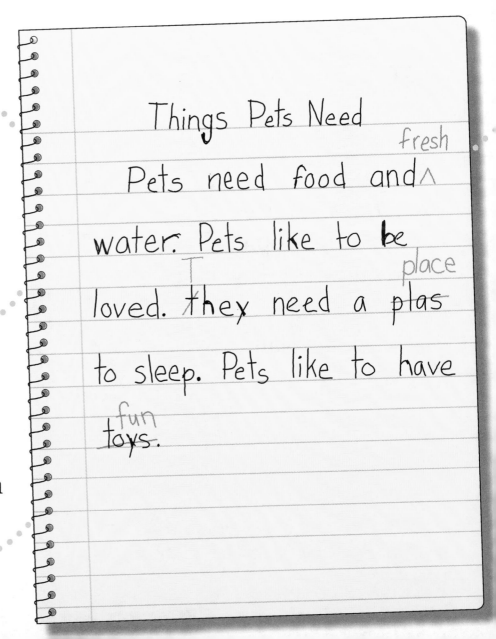

Things Pets Need

Pets need food and ∧ *fresh*

water. Pets like to be

loved. they need a plas *place*

to sleep. Pets like to have

toys. *fun*

5

PUBLISH

- Make a neat copy.
- Share it with others.
- Put it in a class book.

Things Pets Need

Pets need food and fresh water. Pets like to be loved. They need a place to sleep. Pets like to have fun.

by Krista

25

Y U A P F X H B E L D S
Y A   Z M

26

Rules for Writing

All writers follow rules. When you follow rules, others can understand your writing. In this section, you will learn about rules for writing sentences, using capital letters, and much more.

Writing Sentences

A **sentence** states a complete thought.
You use sentences to write.

Mom made spaghetti.

- Begin with a capital letter.
- Leave a space between words.
- End with a punctuation mark.

28

Kinds of Sentences

Telling sentence

> Sam ate the spaghetti.

Asking sentence

> Who is Sam?

Feeling sentence

> Sam is my cat!

29

Using Capital Letters

You use **capital letters** in your writing.

The **first word** in a sentence

Bears catch fish.

Names

Sandy   Trout Lake

The word **I**

When can I go fishing?

Making Plurals

Use the **plural** form for a word that means "more than one."

Add **s** for most plurals.

> friend — friends

Add **es** after words ending in *s*, *x*, *ch*, and *sh*.

> glass — glasses   lunch — lunches
> box — boxes   dish — dishes

Change the word for a few plurals.

> child — children   mouse — mice

31

Using Punctuation

Use **punctuation marks** to make your writing easier to read.

Periods go after telling sentences.

> Summer is the best season.

Question marks go after asking sentences.

> When does summer begin?

Exclamation points go after sentences that show strong feeling.

> Wow, it's hot!

Commas are for short stops. Commas keep words and numbers from running together.

> Dear Gram,   June 13, 1999
> I like red, blue, and green.

Apostrophes show left-out letters or ownership.

> Gram can't wear Anna's hat.

Quotation marks go around a speaker's words.

> Hannah said, "I like your new hat."
> Anna answered, "Thank you."

Understanding Our Language

The words we use are called the **parts of speech**. Here are four of the parts of speech.

A **noun** names a person, place, or thing.

friend	park	apple
Dave	Grant Park	McIntosh

A **pronoun** takes the place of a noun.

I	you	he	she	it
me	we	they	them	us

A **verb** shows action or finishes a thought.

> We picked lots of apples.
> The tree was full of red apples.

An **adjective** tells about a noun or pronoun.

> Dad picked the ripe apples.
> I ate the biggest one.

The **Forms** of Writing

Personal Writing

Have you ever gone on a trip to visit someone? Have you ever been to a zoo? Just think of all the fun times you've had and the important things you've done. This section will show you different ways to write about them.

Writing in Journals

A **journal** is your very own place for writing. You can write in your journal every day.

- Write the date.

- Draw a picture if you want to.

38

- Write about things you do and think about.

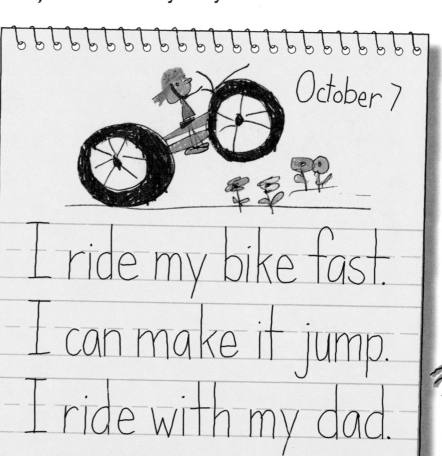

October 7

I ride my bike fast.
I can make it jump.
I ride with my dad.

Ideas for your journal:

- ▶ A story about a friend
- ▶ A wish list
- ▶ Something you like to do
- ▶ A place you like to go
- ▶ A poem
- ▶ Questions you want to ask
- ▶ A joke
- ▶ A list of books you've read

A journal is waiting
for your words.

39

Writing Lists

Lists are easy to write. They can be long or short, serious or silly. You can write lists for many reasons.

- Show what you know.

- Have fun.

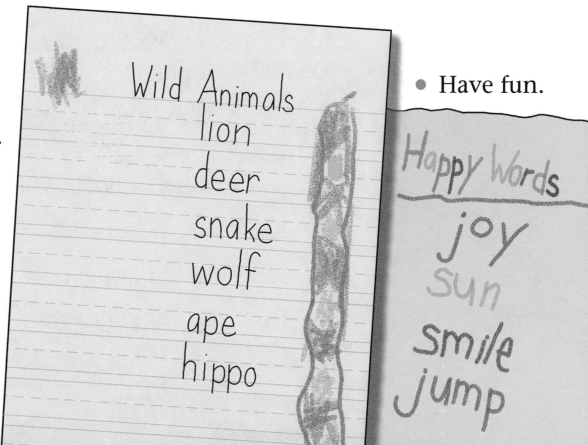

Wild Animals
lion
deer
snake
wolf
ape
hippo

Happy Words
joy
sun
smile
jump

- Remember things.

Store

corn
milk
apples
peanut butter

Some lists you can write:

▸ Favourite things
▸ Pets
▸ Games
▸ Words
▸ Friends
▸ Things to do
▸ Colours

41

Writing Friendly Notes

Writing a **friendly note** is fun. Your note can be an invitation or a thank-you.

An Invitation

Lea,
You are funny.
Do you want to
play at my house?
Say YES.
Michelle

A Thank-You Note

Hi Michelle,
I had fun at your house. Thanks for the ladybug pin.

Lea

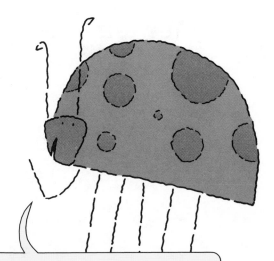

Other notes
can say . . .

▶ Friendly things
▶ Kind things
▶ Funny things

43

Writing Friendly Letters

You can write a **friendly letter** to someone near or far away.

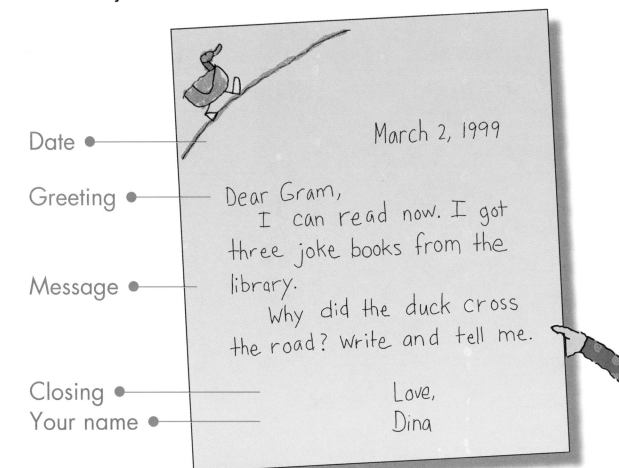

Date

Greeting

Message

Closing
Your name

March 2, 1999

Dear Gram,
    I can read now. I got three joke books from the library.
    Why did the duck cross the road? Write and tell me.

Love,
Dina

Sending Your Letter

Address the envelope. Then send your letter.

Your address

Stamp

SANJ BABOOLAL
440 OAK ST
TORONTO, ON M4K 1C6

CANADA

MRS JUDITH MURPHY
86 FIRST AVE
CALGARY, AB T3E 4M2

Mailing address

POST

45

Writing Stories About Me

A **story about me** is about a special time in your life. A cluster can help you plan your story.

A Cluster

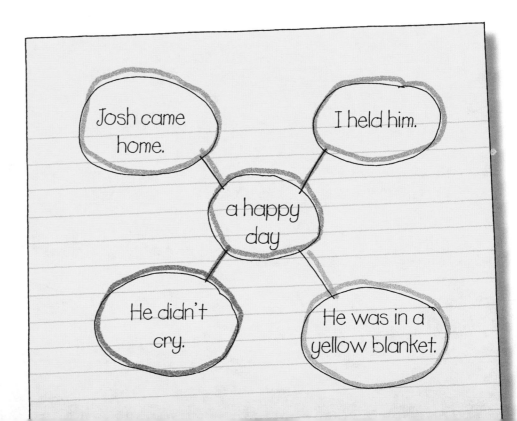

A Story

A Happy Day

One day baby Josh came home. He was in a yellow blanket. My mom let me hold him. He was blowing bubbles. He didn't cry.
by Jesse

47

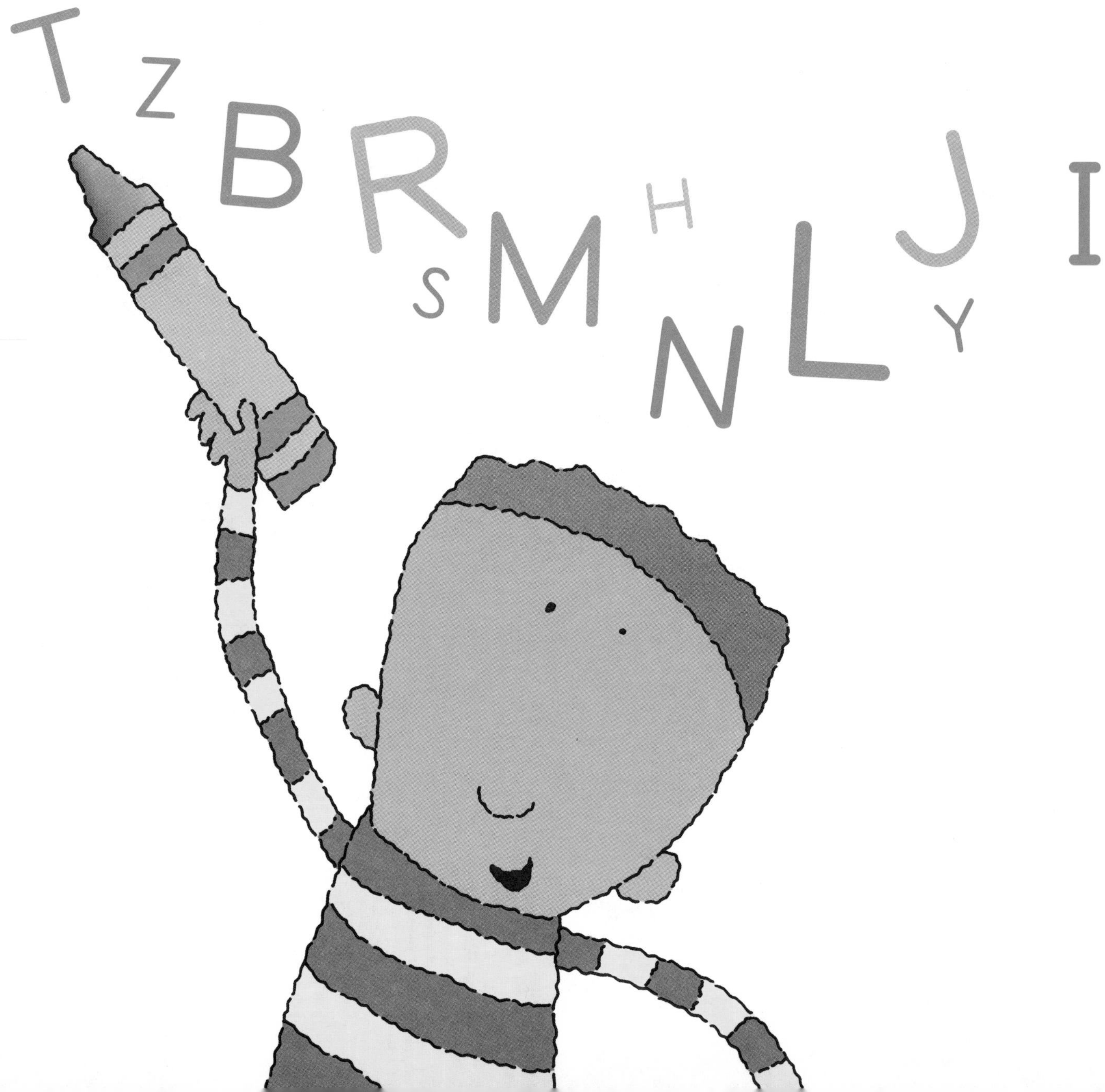

Subject Writing

Writing about other subjects can be just as much fun as writing about yourself. You can write about different people, places, books, and much more. This section will show you how.

Writing About Others

Do you know someone you can write about?
Start with an important idea about this person.
Then write details telling about your idea.

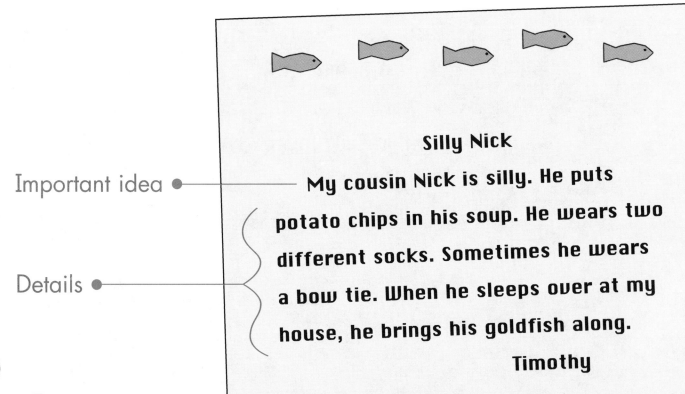

Important idea ●

Details ●

Silly Nick

My cousin Nick is silly. He puts potato chips in his soup. He wears two different socks. Sometimes he wears a bow tie. When he sleeps over at my house, he brings his goldfish along.

Timothy

Write about . . .
▸ A special friend
▸ A favourite aunt
▸ A funny neighbour
▸ A famous person
▸ Your babysitter

51

Writing a Description

You can write **descriptions** about people, places, or things.

- Tell how something looks.

- Tell how something feels.

Our New Car

Our new car is green.
It has a sunroof.
It has soft tan seats.
It is sporty.
My dad thinks it's cool.

52

Use Your Senses

Pick words that tell how something or someone looks, feels, tastes, smells, or sounds.

My Grandma

My grandma
sings a lot.
She smells like
peppermint.

- Tell how someone sounds.

- Tell how someone smells.

Writing Directions

When you write **directions**, you tell the steps for doing something. Use *words* or *numbers* to put the steps in order.

Starting with Words

First •————— First, pour some milk in a glass.

Next •————— Next, put 2 spoons of chocolate syrup in.

Then •————— Then, stir it for 1 minute.

Last •————— Last, drink it. Yum!

Making Chocolate Milk

Michael

54

Starting with Numbers

1. ●
2. ●
3. ●
4. ●

Getting Ready for School
by Betsy

1. Wash up and get dressed.
2. Eat breakfast.
3. Brush your teeth.
4. Grab your schoolbag and go.

Other directions you can write:
- ▶ Taking care of a pet
- ▶ Making breakfast
- ▶ Making a friend

55

Writing Captions

Adding **captions** to pictures makes them more interesting.

We love reading time.

Journals go everywhere!

MIGRATION

Butterflies move from place to place.

Captions give you special information.

Writing About Books

Reading books is fun. Writing about books is fun, too. You can write a poem, make a poster, and do many other things.

Write a poem.

Book _Three Ducks Went Wandering_

by _Ron Roy_

One sunny day
the ducks ran away.
They wanted to play.

Make a poster.

READ

Sheep Out to Eat

by Nancy Shaw

It's very funny.
The sheep like green
food the best.

You can also tell about the books you read.

Do a retelling.

- Tell important parts and favourite parts.

Do a dramatic reading.

- Read favourite parts and funny parts.

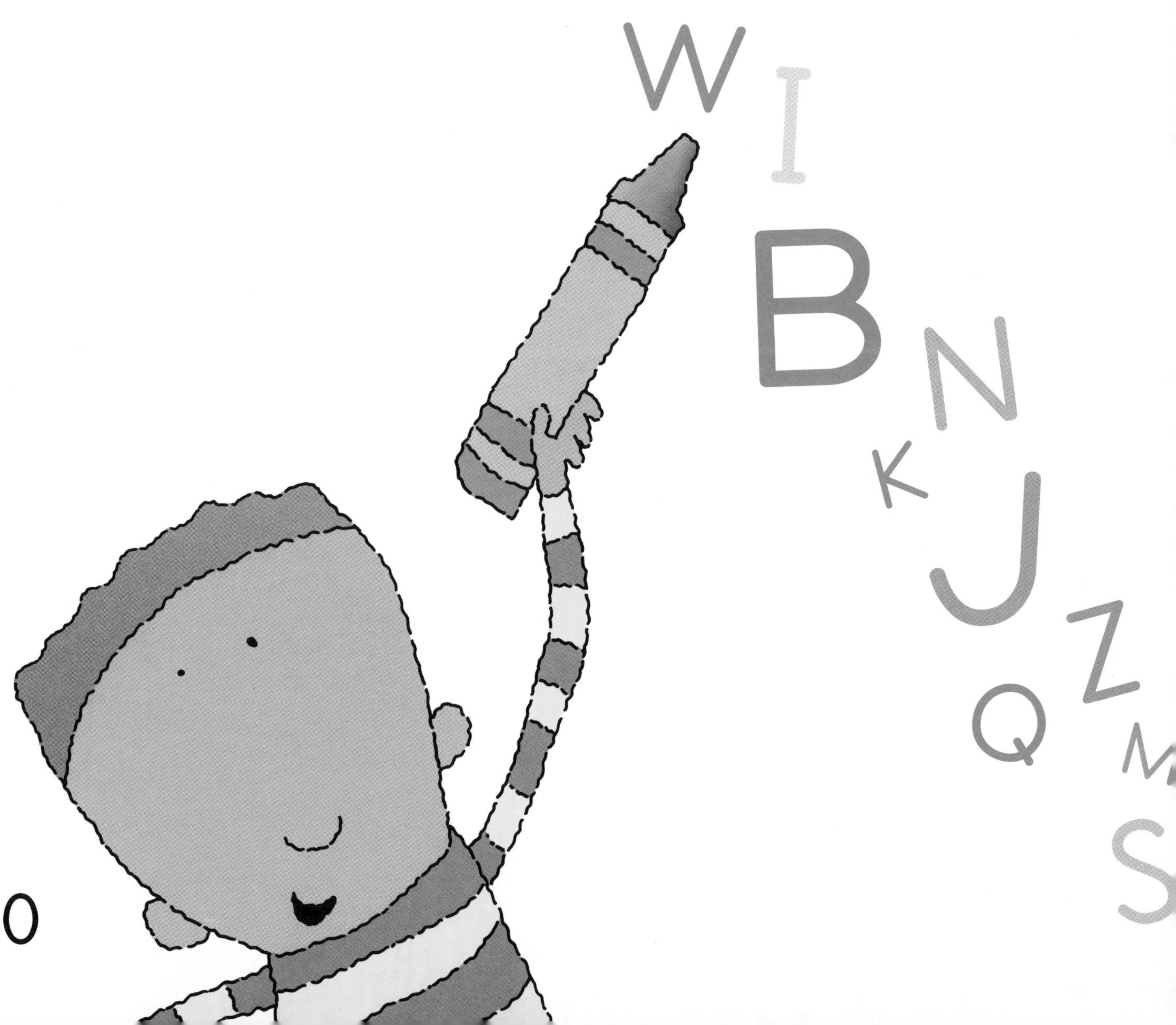

Research Writing

It's fun to explore new things. Research means reading and learning about new and interesting things. It is exciting to write about these things, too. This section will show you how.

Writing Reports

When you learn a lot about a subject, you can write about it in a **report**.

PLAN

- Learn about your topic.
- List or cluster the important facts.

62

2

WRITE

- Use your list or cluster to help you write.
- Write sentences about the topic.
- Spell words the best you can.

Spiders have eight legs. Spiders have fangs. Some spiders are poisonous. Spiders spin webs. Some spiders live undrgrowd. Did you know that spiders aren't insects.

63

3

REVISE

- Read it aloud.
- Does it sound right?
- Make changes.

4

CHECK

- Capitals
- Punctuation
- Spelling

Spiders have eight legs.

Spiders have ^two fangs. Some

spiders are poisonous.

^Most Spiders spin webs. Some

spiders live ~~undrgrowd~~ underground.

Did you know that

spiders aren't insects.?

5

PUBLISH

- Make a neat copy.
- Tell about it.
- Share it with others.

April 21

Spiders

Spiders have eight legs. Spiders have two fangs. Some spiders are poisonous. Most spiders spin webs. Some spiders live underground. Did you know that spiders aren't insects?

by Todd

65

Making Alphabet Books

Making an **alphabet book** is as easy as ABC. You can make one by yourself or with your class.

- Choose a topic.
- List words about the topic for the letters of the alphabet.

Words About Our School

A	art	G	gym
B	bus	H	heart
C	calendar	I	ice cream
D	dancing	J	jokes
E	Eastview	K	kindness
F	friends	L	lunch

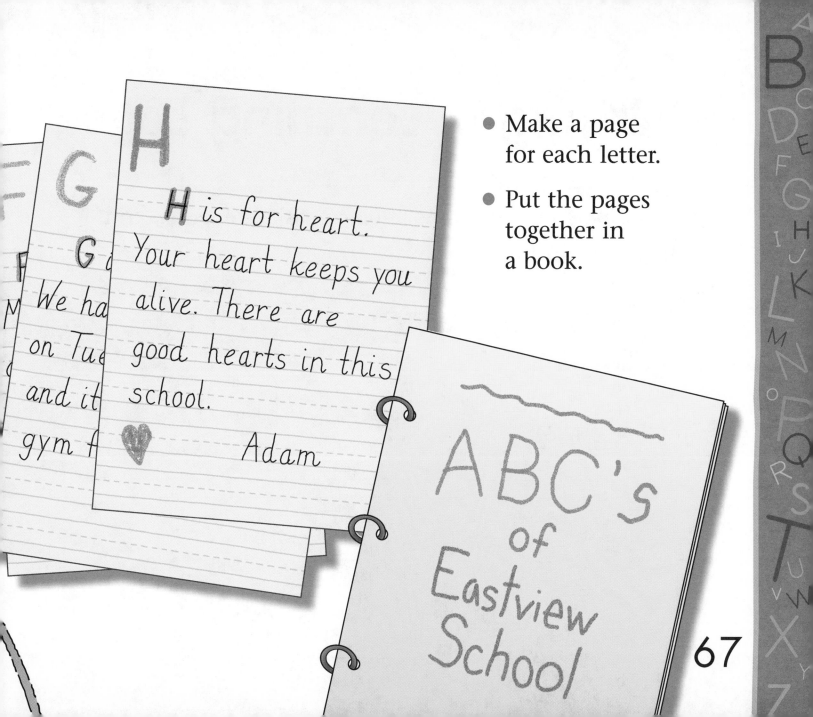

H H is for heart. Your heart keeps you alive. There are good hearts in this school.

Adam

F

G G ...
We ha...
on Tue...
and it...
gym f...

- Make a page for each letter.
- Put the pages together in a book.

ABC'S of Eastview School

67

A B C D E F G H I J K L M N O P Q R S T U V W X Y Z

Writing in Learning Logs

You can write about your school work in a **learning log**. You can write facts, ask questions, and list new words.

A Science Learning Log

Day 1
Today we put seeds in dirt. We put water on top. We hope a plant will grow.

Day 2
The dirt looks black. It smells like outside.

Day 5
A little plant is popping out. Ms. Hill read us a plant book. Plants need sun, air, and water.

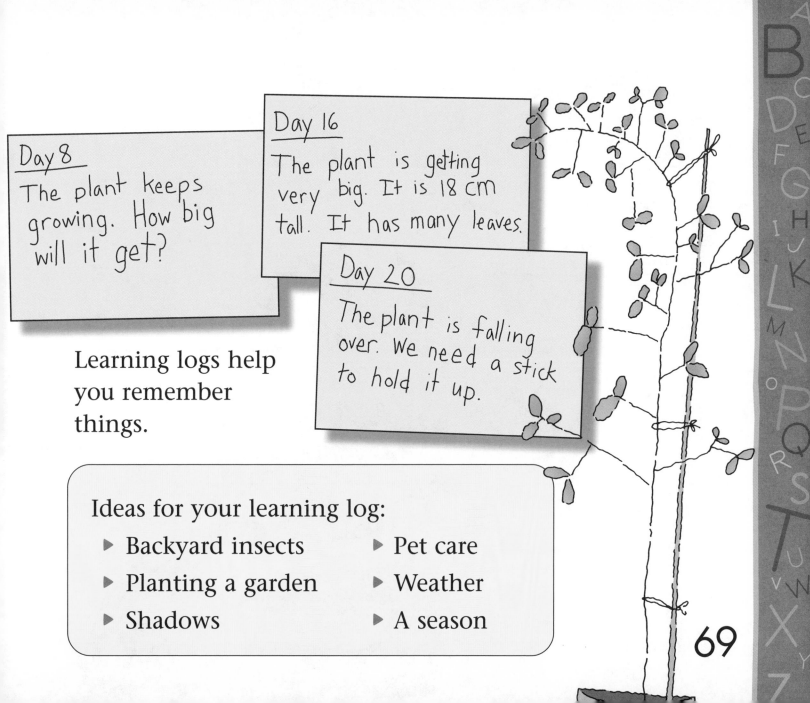

Day 8

The plant keeps growing. How big will it get?

Day 16

The plant is getting very big. It is 18 cm tall. It has many leaves.

Day 20

The plant is falling over. We need a stick to hold it up.

Learning logs help you remember things.

Ideas for your learning log:

- ▸ Backyard insects
- ▸ Planting a garden
- ▸ Shadows
- ▸ Pet care
- ▸ Weather
- ▸ A season

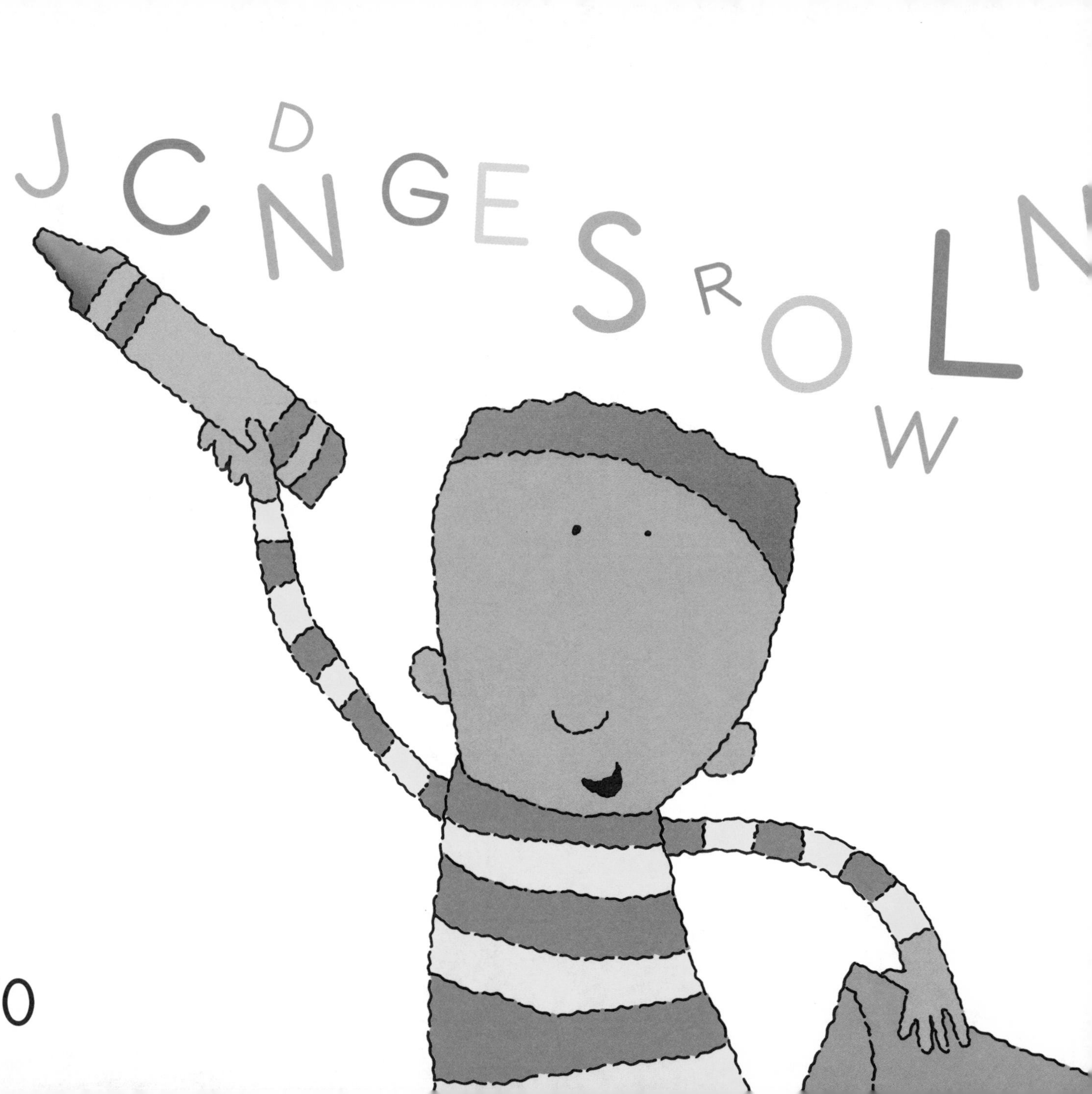

Story and Poetry Writing

You have read or listened to many make-believe stories and poems. You may even know some of them by heart. Would you like to write some of your own? This section will help you get started.

71

Writing Stories

With a little planning, writing a made-up story is easy—and a lot of fun! Here are two ways to plan a story.

You can **plan** a story by answering questions.

- Who are my characters?
- What will happen to my characters?

You can **plan** a story by drawing a picture.

- Try telling the story in your picture before you write it.

72

Jake used a picture to plan his story. His story has a beginning, a middle, and an ending.

Pumpkin the Cat

by Jake

Beginning

Middle

Ending

One sunny day Pumpkin the cat sat on a rock. The rock moved! It was a turtle! Pumpkin got so scared, she ran away. She didn't come back until late at night. She never sat on a green rock again.

73

Writing Poems

Writing poems is like making little word pictures. Think of the best words to use in your poems.

Couplet

- Write **two** lines that rhyme.

> Sometimes comets in space
> Look like they're having a race.
> – Max

Triplet

- Write **three** lines that rhyme.

> Colours, colours everywhere,
> Colours here and colours there,
> Colours on the shirt I wear.
> – Shiere

Quatrain

- Write **four** lines.
  Make at least two lines rhyme.

Polka dots, polka dots
On my dress.
How many polka dots?
Can you guess?

            – Kathleen

The owl in the tree was talking to me.
I heard him say, "Good night."
My sister says that owls don't talk.
But I know she's not right.

            – Shavonn

More Poem Ideas

Tongue Twister

- Begin most of the words with the **same sound**.

> Jackson jumped
> and jammed
> just like Michael
> Jordan.

Cinquain

- Write **five** lines. Use the form below.

One word (the topic)
Two words
Three words
Four words
One word

> Shadow
> Tall, short,
> Hops, waves, jumps.
> Follows where I go.
> Me!

List Poem

- Make a **list**. Here are three list poems.

ABC's

Aunt
Bonnie
Can
Dance
Every
Friday

Ideas

Snow is everywhere.
    Snow is on our school.
    Snow is on the swings.
    Snow is on the trees.
    Snow is on the houses.
    Snow is under our feet.
    Snow is on our noses.
Snow is everywhere!

    – Clarendon School
        Room 11

A name and
describing
words

Joker
On the bus
Silly
Eats cold pizza.

77

Writing with Patterns

You can write songs, poems, and stories that follow a pattern. Most patterns have rhyming words and a special beat.

Song with Pattern

The Itsy Bitsy Spider

The itsy bitsy spider
went up the waterspout.
Down came the rain
and washed the spider out.

Out came the sun
and dried up all the rain.
Then the itsy bitsy spider
Went up the spout again.

Rhyming words

New Song

Once you learn the pattern, write your own words.

The Friendly, Funny Lobster

The friendly, funny lobster
climbed out of the blue sea.
He crawled across the sand
and sat down next to me.

He reached out a claw
and then shook hands with me.
Then the friendly, funny lobster
crept back into the sea.

Here are some more patterns to follow.

- ▸ The Gingerbread Man
- ▸ Over in the Meadow
- ▸ This Old Man
- ▸ Miss Mary Mack

79

Reading
and Word Study

Reading Skills

This section will help you grow as a reader. It gives you tips for thinking about your reading, for reading new words, and much more!

Reading to Understand

Reading takes lots of thinking. You should think before, during, and after reading.

Think Before Reading

LOOK over your reading.

- Check the title.
- Look at the pictures.

PREDICT what will be in the reading.

Think During Reading

TRY to picture what you are reading about.

CHECK to see if your predictions are right or wrong.

Think After Reading

TELL yourself or someone else what the reading was about.

ASK for help if you didn't understand part of the reading.

Reading New Words

There are many ways to read new words.

Try these tips for reading new words.

LOOK for clues.

- First read the whole sentence.

- Ask yourself what word would make sense in the sentence.

- Look at the pictures on the page.

LOOK for parts or patterns you know.

- If you can read but, you can read butter and button.

- If you can read hill, you can read will.

- If you can read play, you can read playing.

LISTEN for sounds.

- Say the word slowly and listen for sounds at the beginning, middle, and end.

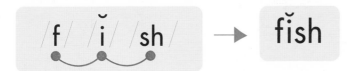

ASK for help.

Using Everyday Words

Everyday words are words you read and write many times a day.

A	B	C
about	baby	called
after	be	can
again	because	car
all	been	children
always	before	come
am	big	could
and	book	**D** did
any	boy	down
are	brother	**E** each
ask	but	eat
away	by	every

86

F family	**H** had	**J** jump
father	happy	just
find	has	**K** keep
first	have	knew
for	he	know
found	help	**L** last
friend	her	left
from	here	let
funny	him	like
G get	his	little
girl	house	live
give	how	long
go	**I** if	look
going	into	love
good	is	

M		O		Q R	
M	made	**O**	of	**Q**	question
	make		off	**R**	ride
	man		old		right
	many		once		room
	me		only		run
	more		or	**S**	said
	mother		other		saw
	must		our		say
	my		out		school
N	name		over		she
	need	**P**	part		sister
	new		people		some
	next		place		something
	night		play		sometimes
	not		please		soon
	now		put		stop

T
take
talk
thank
that
the
their
them
then
there
they
thing
this
time
to
told
took

U
under
until
up
upon
us
use

V
very

W
walk
want
was
way
we
well
went
were
what

when
where
which
who
why
will
with
woman
won't
work
would
write

Y
yes
you
your

Z
zoo

89

Using the Right Word

Words that sound the same but have different meanings are called **homophones**.

ate, eight

> The rabbits ate the carrots.
> I saw eight rabbits in the garden.

for, four

> I made a card for Mom.
> Mom made four cupcakes.

hear, here

I hear Ben's cat.
The cat is here.

know, no

Do you know my name?
"No, I don't," said Theo.

read, red

Kim read a poetry book.
The book has a red cover.

road, rode

> Emma lives on that road.
> She rode her bike home.

son, sun

> Mr. Kitt's son lives in Alberta.
> The sun shines a lot in Alberta.

sum, some

> The sum of 2 + 2 is 4.
> Do you want some grapes?

tail, tale

A beaver has a flat tail.
Sometimes a story is called a tale.

to, two, too

Let's go to the movies.
I'll buy two tickets.
Can we have popcorn, too?

won, one

Brady won a gold medal.
He has a silver one already.

94

Word-Study Skills

We use letters and sounds in our
language. Knowing more about them
will help you read and learn new words.

Aa

alligator

bat
map
Sam

ape

cake
play
rain

96

Bb

butterfly

baby

balloon

bird

book

bow

boy

bug

97

Cc

cup

candle

cat

coat

cereal

cent

circle

city

Dd

duck

daddy
daisy
day
dinner
dinosaur
dog
door

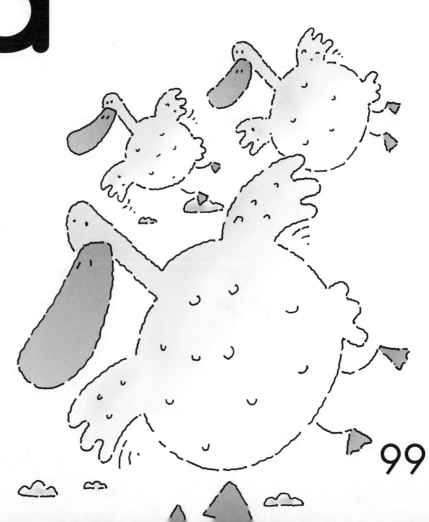

99

E e

eggs

deck
Meg
pen

eagle

bean
Pete
see

Ff

fish

family
father
feet
finger
fire
food
fun

101

Gg

girl

gate
goat
gold

gem

gerbil
giant
giraffe

Hh

hat

hair
hand
head
home
horse
house
hug

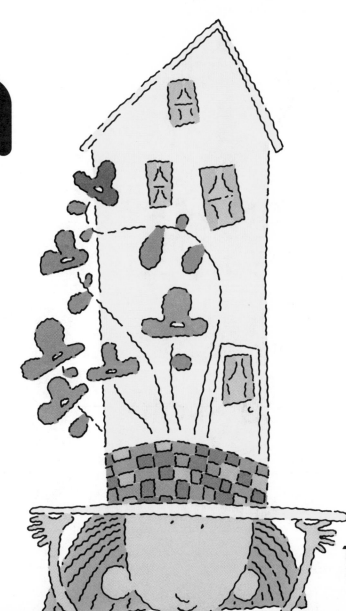

103

Ii

igloo

bib
hill
pig

ice skate

bike
night
pie

104

Jj

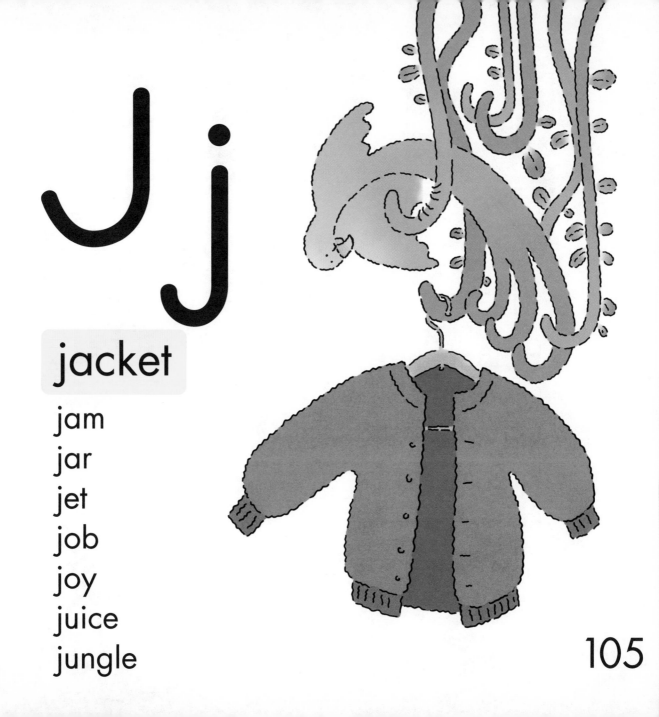

jacket

jam
jar
jet
job
joy
juice
jungle

105

Kk

kite

kangaroo
key
kid
king
kiss
kitchen
kitten

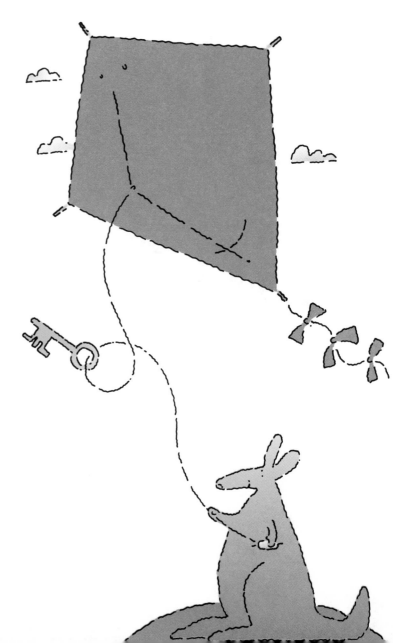

Ll

ladybug

land
laugh
leaf
leg
letter
light
love

Mm

mouse

mammal

man

mask

milk

moon

morning

mother

Nn

nest

name
necklace
neighbour
nickel
night
nose
nurse

O o

octopus

box

dog

rock

oak tree

bone

goat

no

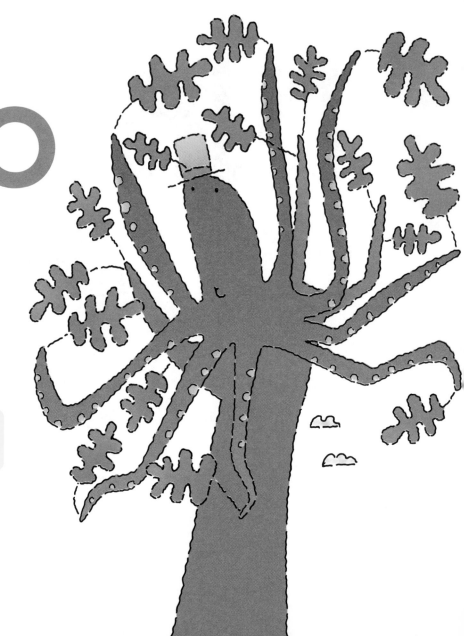

P p

penguin

paper
party
pencil
people
pet
picture
popcorn

111

Qq

quilt

quart
quarter
queen
question
question mark
quiet
quiz

112

Rr

rocket

rabbit
rain
rat
ring
road
room
rose

S s

socks

sailboat
sand
seed
sister
soap
song
sun

T t

turtle

table
teacher
television
today
tooth
toy
turkey

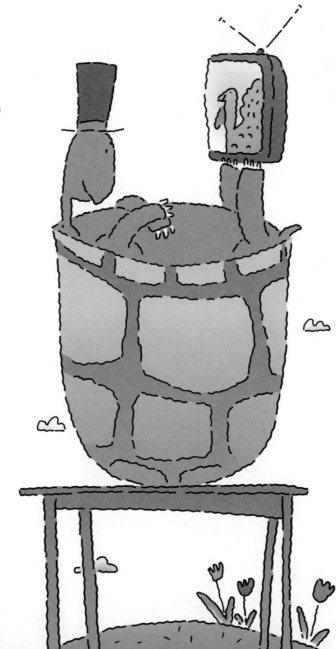

115

Uu

umbrella

duck
fun
rug

unicycle

mule
Sue
suit

116

Vv

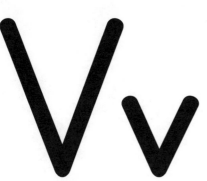

vase

valentine
vegetable
vest
vine
violin
visit
voice

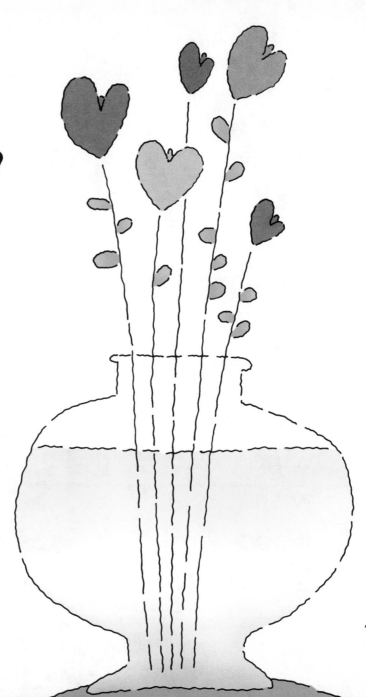

117

Ww

wagon

water
wind
window
wing
wish
wood
worm

X x

bo<u>x</u>

axe
fix
fox
Max
ox
six
wax

119

Y y

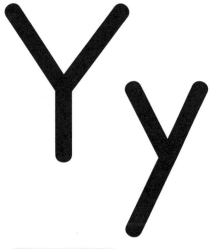

yarn

yard
year
you
yo-yo

Sometimes y is a vowel.

Happy and **fly**
have the vowel y.

Zz

zipper

zebra

zero

zigzag

zone

zoo

zucchini

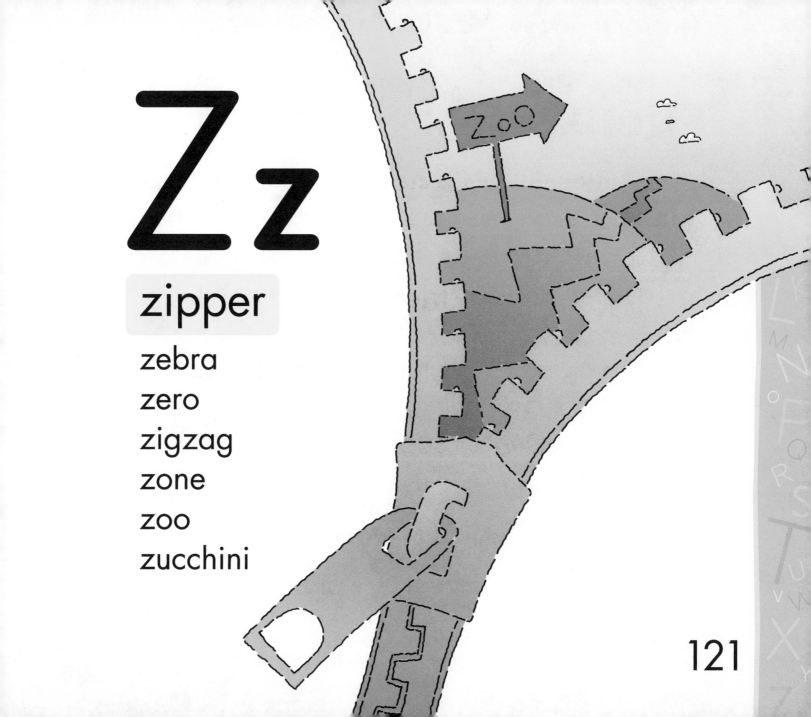

Consonant Blends

Consonant blends are two or more consonants that come together and keep their own sounds.

fr • pr • dr	friends	pretty	dress
bl • cl • fl	blue	cloud	flag
sp • st • sn	spot	step	snow

Blends at the end of words:

de<u>sk</u>   be<u>st</u>   pi<u>nk</u>

122

Consonant Digraphs

Consonant digraphs are two consonants that come together and make one sound.

ch	child	chop	chick
sh	ship	shop	shell
th	thank	this	thirty
wh	why	when	wheel

Digraphs at the end of words:

cat<u>ch</u>   ma<u>th</u>   wi<u>sh</u>

Short Vowels

Most words with short vowel sounds have this pattern:

| consonant - vowel - consonant | → | sŭn |

short ă	short ĕ	short ĭ	short ŏ	short ŭ
map	bell	pin	hop	bug
pan	pen	ship	Mom	gum

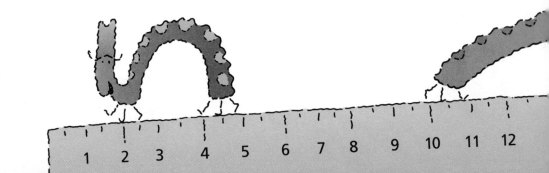

Long Vowels

Here are two patterns for long vowel sounds:

consonant - vowel - consonant + e → cāke

consonant - vowel - vowel - consonant → sōap

long ā	long ē	long ī	long ō	long ū
tape	Pete	bike	rope	mule
rain	leaf	pies	boat	suit

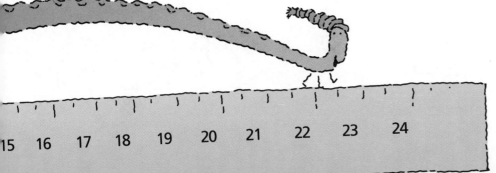

15 16 17 18 19 20 21 22 23 24

125

Rhyming Families

Rhyming helps you read and write new words.

**If you know
these words,** **you can read and write these.**

hat	bat	sat	flat

fun	run	bun	sun

mop	top	hop	crop

If you know these words, you can read and write these.

fish	wish	dish	swish
cake	lake	bake	snake
like	bike	hike	Mike
rain	pain	train	grain

127

Contractions

A **contraction** is one shorter word made from two words. You leave some letters out.

Two Words	Contraction	Two Words	Contraction
are not	aren't	has not	hasn't
cannot	can't	I will	I'll
did not	didn't	it is	it's
do not	don't	you are	you're

Compound Words

A **compound word** is a longer word made from two shorter words.

Two Words		Compound Word
base + ball	=	baseball
fish + hook	=	fishhook
pop + corn	=	popcorn
snow + flake	=	snowflake
space + ship	=	spaceship

The Student
Almanac

Helpful Words, Maps, and Lists

You'll love using these pages about theme words, maps, math, computers, and handwriting. This section covers all of these subjects.

Using Theme Words

This chapter includes word lists for important themes you will study in school.

Themes

- ▸ Calendar Words
- ▸ Numbers and Colours
- ▸ Seasons and Weather
- ▸ Places
- ▸ Plants
- ▸ Food Pyramid
- ▸ Animals
- ▸ Five Senses

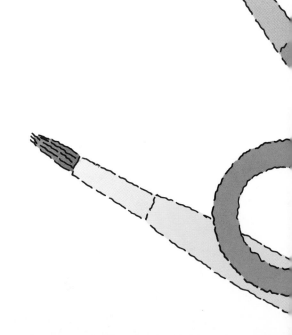

132

Calendar Words

The name of each **month** and **day** begins with a capital letter.

January
February
March
April
May
June
July
August
September
October
November
December

Sunday
Monday
Tuesday
Wednesday
Thursday
Friday
Saturday

133

Numbers and Colours

Numbers and colours are everywhere!

four

three

two

4

one

3

blue

2

green

yellow

zero

1

orange

0

red

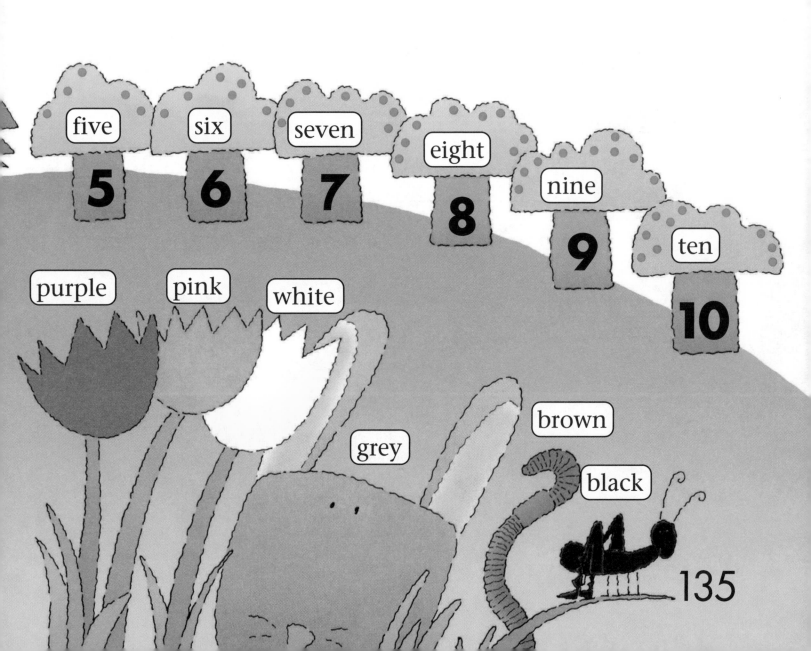

five **5**

six **6**

seven **7**

eight **8**

nine **9**

ten **10**

purple

pink

white

grey

brown

black

135

Seasons and Weather

There are four seasons in a year. Each season has a different kind of weather. You use special words when you talk and write about the seasons and the weather.

Seasons

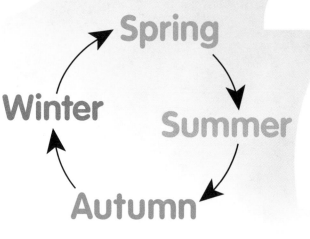

Spring

Summer

Autumn

Winter

Weather Words

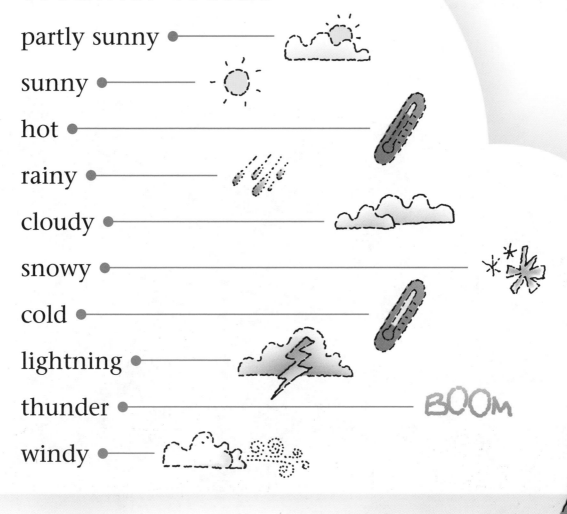

partly sunny

sunny

hot

rainy

cloudy

snowy

cold

lightning

thunder

BOOM

windy

Places

Going places is fun!

beach

tundra

prairie

mountains

hills

river

valley

forest

path

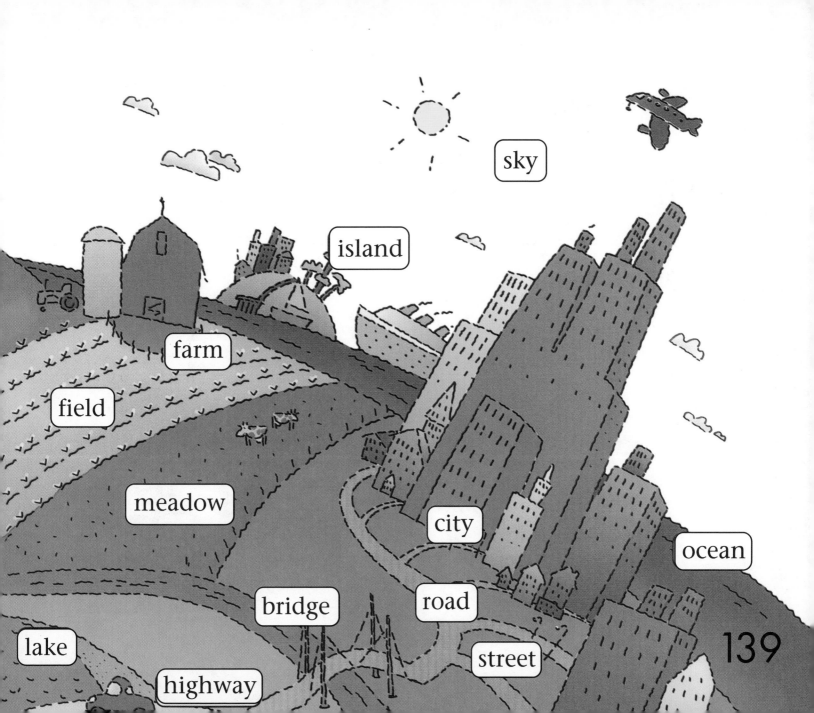

sky

island

farm

field

meadow

city

ocean

bridge

road

lake

street

highway

139

Plants

Many kinds of plants grow on earth. Garden flowers and leafy trees are two kinds of plants. These plants need sunlight, water, air, and soil to grow.

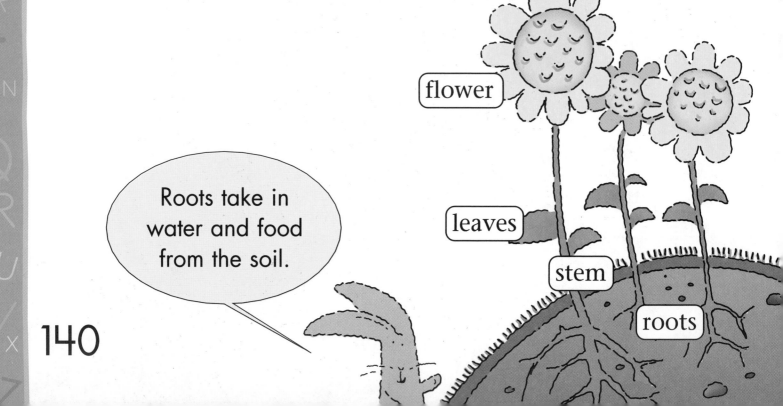

Roots take in water and food from the soil.

flower

leaves

stem

roots

141

Food Pyramid

A food pyramid shows you how to eat right to be healthy.

Eat more foods from the bottom and fewer foods from the top.

meat, fish, beans, eggs, nuts •

fruits •

bread, cereal, rice, pasta •

142

fats, oils, sweets

milk, yogurt, cheese

vegetables

143

Animals of the . . .

Oceans	Woodlands	Grasslands
crab	bear	antelope
fish	beaver	elephant
octopus	chipmunk	giraffe
shark	deer	hippopotamus
starfish	porcupine	lion
stingray	raccoon	prairie dog
whale	skunk	zebra
	squirrel	

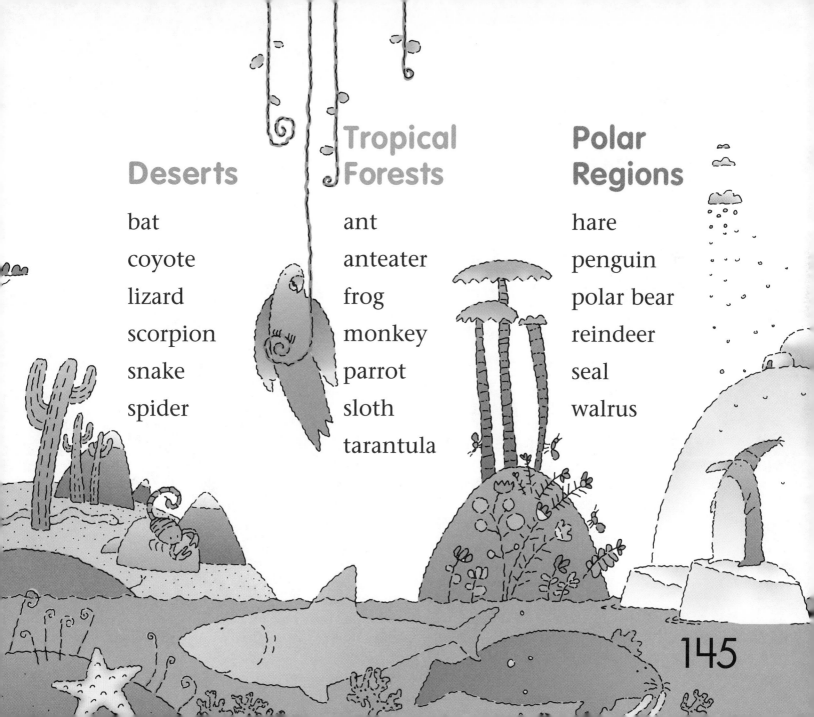

Deserts

bat
coyote
lizard
scorpion
snake
spider

Tropical Forests

ant
anteater
frog
monkey
parrot
sloth
tarantula

Polar Regions

hare
penguin
polar bear
reindeer
seal
walrus

Five Senses

I discover the world with my senses.

I **hear** with my ears,
I **taste** with my tongue,
I **see** with my eyes
    by the light of the sun.
I **touch** with my hands,
    along with my toes,
And whatever I **smell**
    tickles my nose.

147

Using Maps

Maps help you find places near and far.

Map Signs

Most maps show directions. **N** is for **North**, **E** is for **East**, **S** is for **South**, and **W** is for **West**.

A **legend** explains the symbols on a map.

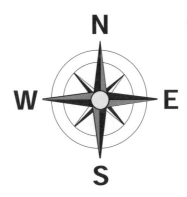

CANADA

⭐ National Capital

★ Provincial/Territorial Capitals

–·–·– Provincial/Territorial Boundary

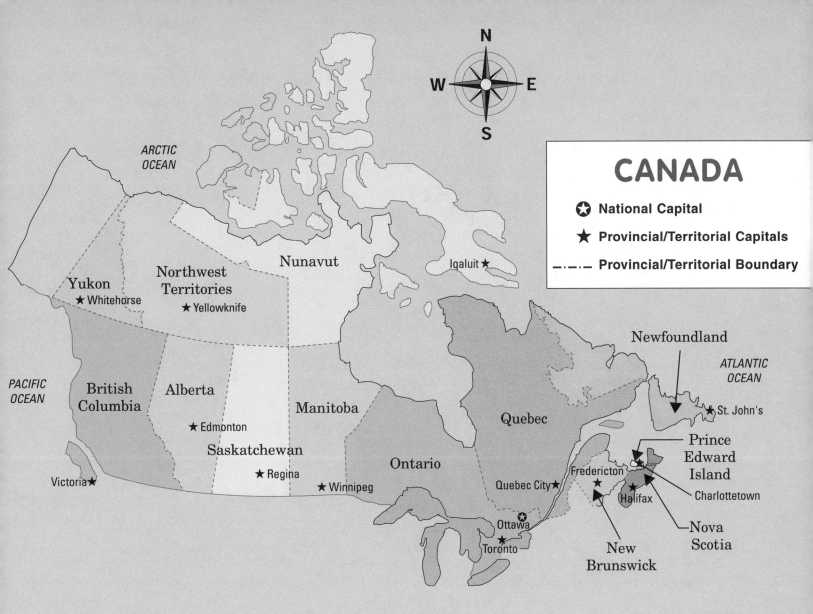

N
W **E**
S

ARCTIC
OCEAN

CANADA

⭐ National Capital

★ Provincial/Territorial Capitals

—·—·— Provincial/Territorial Boundary

Nunavut

Iqaluit ★

Yukon
★ Whitehorse

Northwest
Territories
★ Yellowknife

Newfoundland

ATLANTIC
OCEAN

PACIFIC
OCEAN

British
Columbia

Alberta

★ Edmonton

Saskatchewan

★ Regina

Manitoba

Quebec

St. John's ★

Prince
Edward
Island

Ontario

Fredericton
★

Charlottetown

Victoria ★

★ Winnipeg

Quebec City ★

Halifax
★

Ottawa ✪

Toronto
★

New
Brunswick

Nova
Scotia

149

ARCTIC
OCEAN

ALASKA
(U.S.)

GREENLAND

N

W   E

S

CANADA

North America

PACIFIC
OCEAN

UNITED STATES

ATLANTIC
OCEAN

MEXICO

Gulf of
Mexico

WEST INDIES

150

CENTRAL
AMERICA

SOUTH AMERICA

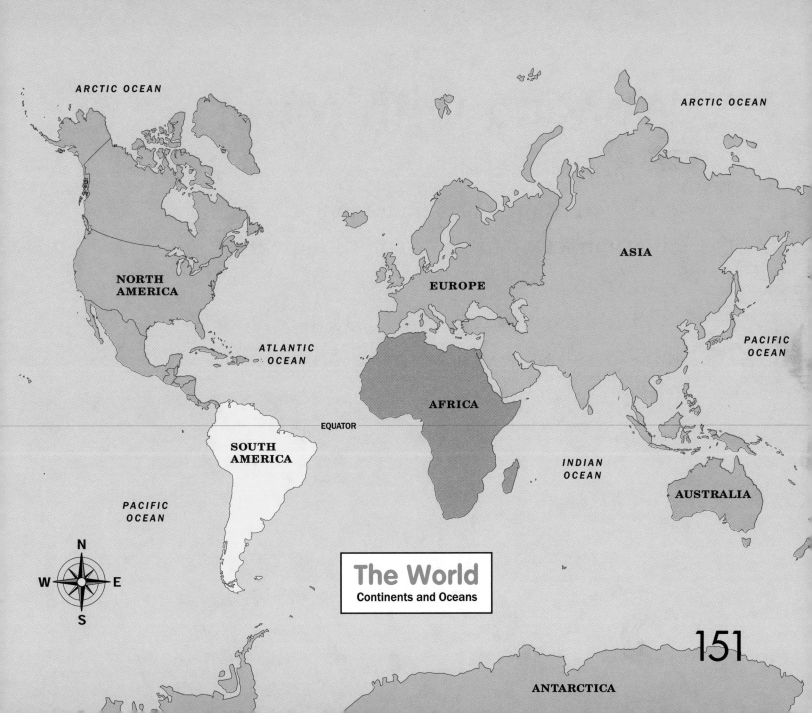

ARCTIC OCEAN

ARCTIC OCEAN

NORTH
AMERICA

ASIA

EUROPE

ATLANTIC
OCEAN

PACIFIC
OCEAN

AFRICA

EQUATOR

SOUTH
AMERICA

INDIAN
OCEAN

PACIFIC
OCEAN

AUSTRALIA

N
W   E
S

The World
Continents and Oceans

151

ANTARCTICA

Working with Math

You work with math every day. You tell time. You count your lunch money. You add and subtract when you share things with your friends.

In this section you will find charts and tables to show you how math can work for you.

Telling Time

Face clocks show time with hands pointing to numbers. **Digital clocks** show time with numbers. Both of these clocks show 2:30.

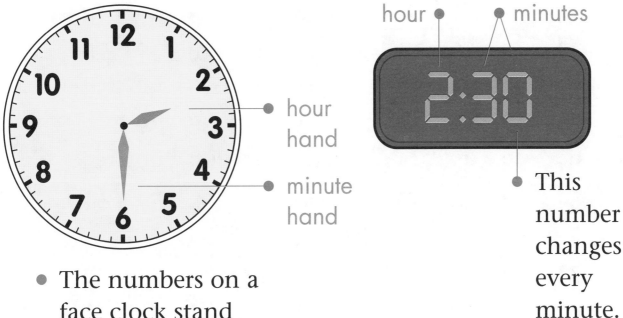

hour

minutes

hour hand

minute hand

This number changes every minute.

- The numbers on a face clock stand for both hours and minutes.

153

Numbers 1 to 100

The chart below will help you count by 1's, 5's, and 10's.

Hundred Chart

1	2	3	4	5	6	7	8	9	10
11	12	13	14	15	16	17	18	19	20
21	22	23	24	25	26	27	28	29	30
31	32	33	34	35	36	37	38	39	40
41	42	43	44	45	46	47	48	49	50
51	52	53	54	55	56	57	58	59	60
61	62	63	64	65	66	67	68	69	70
71	72	73	74	75	76	77	78	79	80
81	82	83	84	85	86	87	88	89	90
91	92	93	94	95	96	97	98	99	100

Place Value

This chart shows what each part of a number is worth.

hundreds	tens	ones		
		7	=	7
	1	0	=	10
	3	2	=	32
	5	5	=	55
1	0	0	=	100

7 = 0 hundreds	0 tens	7 ones
10 = 0 hundreds	1 tens	0 ones
32 = 0 hundreds	3 tens	2 ones
55 = 0 hundreds	5 tens	5 ones
100 = 1 hundreds	0 tens	0 ones

Bar Graphs

A **bar graph** helps you show how many.

Children's Favourite Season

spring = 5
summer = 9
autumn = 4
winter = 7

Money

 =

one dollar = four quarters

one dollar = 10 dimes (count by 10's)

one dollar = 20 nickels (count by 5's)

one dollar = 100 pennies (count by 1's)

157

Addition and Subtraction

Addition means putting numbers together.

●●●● ●●

$$4 + 2 = 6$$

sum

● This says four plus two equals six.

Subtraction means taking numbers away.

✗✗✗✗●●

$$6 - 4 = 2$$

difference

● This says six minus four equals two.

Fractions

A **fraction** is a part of something whole.

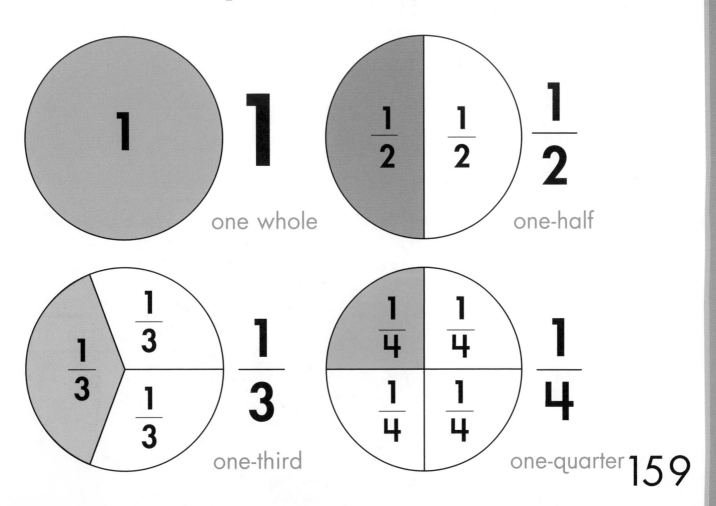

1 — one whole

$\frac{1}{2}$ — one-half

$\frac{1}{3}$ — one-third

$\frac{1}{4}$ — one-quarter

159

Knowing About a Computer

The more you know about a computer, the more you can do with it. You can use a computer for writing and many other things.

Parts of a Personal Computer

Silly Nick

My cousin Nick is silly. He puts potato chips in his soup. He wears two different socks. Sometimes he wears a bow tie. When he sleeps over at my house, he brings his goldfish along.

Timothy

printer

mouse

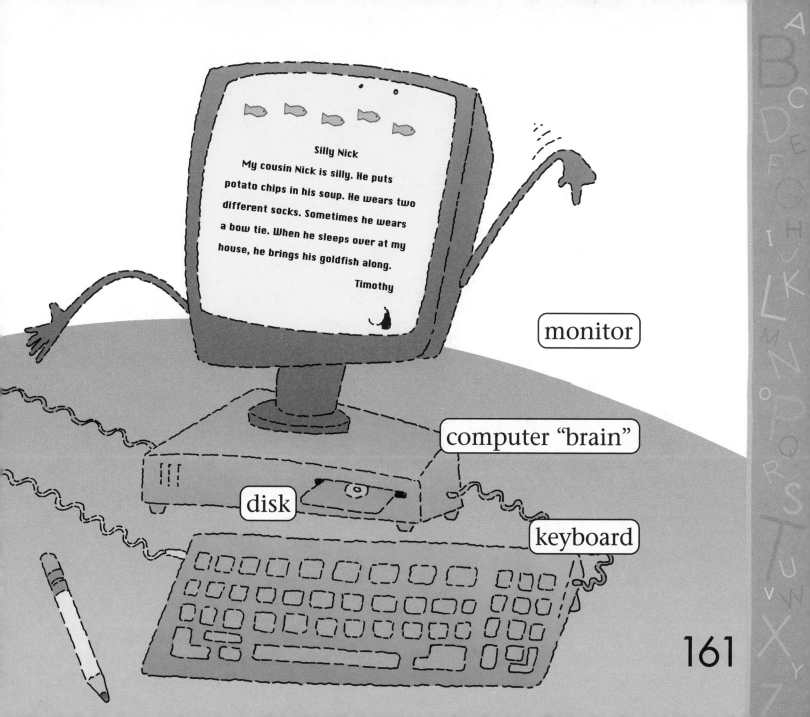

Silly Nick
My cousin Nick is silly. He puts potato chips in his soup. He wears two different socks. Sometimes he wears a bow tie. When he sleeps over at my house, he brings his goldfish along.

Timothy

monitor

computer "brain"

disk

keyboard

161

Practising Handwriting

Neat handwriting helps you and others read and enjoy your writing.

Handwriting Hints

- Look at handwriting models.
- Practise letters often.
- Leave spaces between words.
- Slant all letters the same way.

162

Manuscript Models

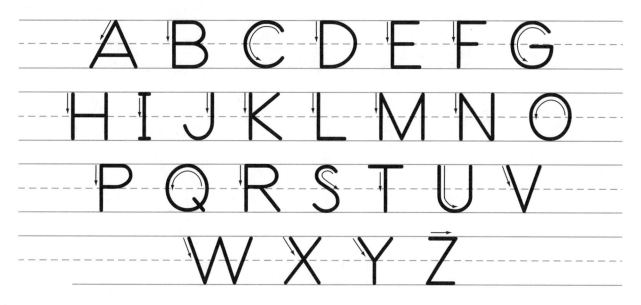

A B C D E F G
H I J K L M N O
P Q R S T U V
W X Y Z

a b c d e f g h i j
k l m n o p q r s
t u v w x y z

163

Continuous Stroke Models

A B C D E F G
H I J K L M N O
P Q R S T U V
W X Y Z

a b c d e f g h i j
k l m n o p q r s
t u v w x y z

Index

The **index** can help you find information in your handbook. Let's say you want to write a letter. You can look in your index under "letters" for help.

T

U

V

W